Clara
Barton

A Buddy Book
by
Christy DeVillier

ABDO
Publishing Company

VISIT US AT

www.abdopub.com

Published by ABDO Publishing Company, 4940 Viking Drive, Suite 622, Edina, Minnesota 55435. Copyright © 2004 by Abdo Consulting Group, Inc. International copyrights reserved in all countries. No part of this book may be reproduced in any form without written permission from the publisher.

Printed in the United States.

Edited by: Michael P. Goecke
Contributing Editor: Matt Ray
Image Research: Deborah Coldiron
Graphic Design: Jane Halbert
Cover Photograph: Library of Congress
Interior Photographs/Illustrations: Fotosearch, Hulton Archives, North Wind

Library of Congress Cataloging-in-Publication Data

Devillier, Christy, 1971-
    Clara Barton / Christy Devillier.
       v. cm. — (First biographies)
    Includes bibliographical references and index.
    Contents: Who is Clara Barton?—Growing up—Teaching—Civil War—Missing soldiers—The Red Cross—A life of helping others.
    ISBN 1-59197-511-5
    1. Barton, Clara, 1821-1912—Juvenile literature. 2. Red Cross—United States—Biography—Juvenile literature. 3. Nurses—United States—Biography.
    4. American Red Cross—Juvenile literature. [1. Barton, Clara, 1821-1912.
    2. Nurses. 3. American National Red Cross. 4. Women—Biography.] I. Title.

HV569.B3D48 2004
361.7'634'092—dc22
[B]
                                                                    2003052264

Table Of Contents

Who Is Clara Barton?

Clara Barton is a famous humanitarian. She nursed soldiers during the American Civil War. Clara Barton also started the American Red Cross. The Red Cross helps others in times of need.

Clara Barton

The Red Cross flag is white with a red cross.

5

Growing Up

Clarissa Barton was born on December 25, 1821. Her family called her Clara. Clara had four older brothers and sisters. Her father was a farmer. The Barton family lived in New Oxford, Massachusetts.

Young Clara was shy. But she enjoyed school. She studied math, history, poetry, and other subjects.

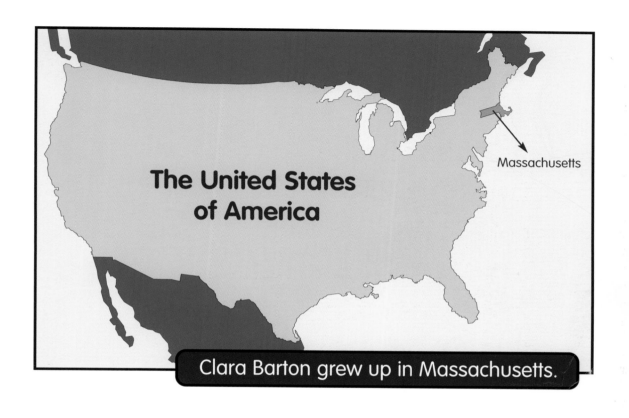

The United States
of America

Massachusetts

Clara Barton grew up in Massachusetts.

Young Clara liked riding horses.
Her brother David taught her to
ride horses bareback.

One day, Clara's brother David fell. Afterward, he had a fever and headaches. Clara began taking care of her brother. She was only 11 years old. Clara nursed David for about two years.

Teaching

In 1839, Clara Barton began teaching school. She was 17 years old. Clara taught students in a one-room schoolhouse. Her students were different ages.

Small one-room schoolhouses were common in the 1800s.

Clara taught school for many years. In 1850, she decided to become a student again. She moved to Clinton, New York. Clara began studying at the Clinton Liberal Institute. She studied French, German, science, and other subjects.

Clara left school when her mother died in 1851. One year later, she moved to Bordentown, New Jersey. She opened a free public school. Clara taught there for two years.

Civil War

The American Civil War broke out in 1861. At this time, Clara Barton lived in Washington, D.C. She worked at the U.S. Patent Office.

Northern states fought the Southern states during the American Civil War.

Clara saw that there were not enough supplies for hurt soldiers. So, she began gathering food and clothes. Clara asked friends and neighbors to donate money. Clara asked for donations in a newspaper ad. She also asked families of soldiers to help. Soldiers were thankful for Clara's supplies.

The First Battle of Bull Run was the first great battle of the Civil War. It took place near Washington, D.C. Hurt soldiers filled the city. Clara worked hard to help them.

The First Battle of Bull Run broke out in July 1861.

Clara wanted to go to the battlefield to help hurt soldiers. At first, officials would not let her go. They believed that the battlefield was no place for an unmarried woman. Clara told them she had wagons of supplies to give out. At last, they let her go.

Clara brought supplies to Culpeper, Virginia, in August 1862. She nursed many hurt soldiers.

Clara nursed soldiers throughout the Civil War. Thankful soldiers began calling Clara the "Angel of the Battlefield."

Clara Barton, the "Angel of the Battlefield"

Missing Soldiers

In 1865, there were many missing Civil War soldiers. Their families did not know what happened to them. Some soldiers had died and were buried in unmarked graves. Other soldiers were prisoners of war.

Clara Barton began a search for the missing soldiers. She set up an office in Annapolis, Maryland. Families of missing soldiers wrote to Clara. She helped them discover what had happened to the missing men.

Confederate General Robert E. Lee surrendered on April 9, 1865.

The Civil War ended in 1865. By 1868, Clara Barton had found 22,000 missing soldiers.

The Red Cross

In 1869, Clara Barton traveled to Switzerland. There, she met people who worked for the Red Cross. These people helped others during wartime. They helped hurt soldiers and refugees.

Clara joined the Red Cross. She helped many people during the Franco-Prussian War. Germany gave Clara the Iron Cross of Merit for her hard work.

Clara and the Red Cross helped during the Franco-Prussian War.

Clara Barton wanted to start a Red Cross organization in the United States. She talked to lawmakers about it. Clara spoke to President Rutherford B. Hayes and President James Garfield. Clara made speeches about the Red Cross. She wrote booklets about the Red Cross, too.

Rutherford B. Hayes was the 19th United States president.

Thanks to Clara, the American Red Cross was formed in 1881. Clara became the president.

Clara and the Red Cross helped many people. They aided sufferers of earthquakes, floods, and droughts. The Red Cross gave out food and other needed supplies. They helped people rebuild their towns and cities.

The Red Cross offers aid after many kinds of disasters.

A Life Of Helping Others

Clara Barton left the Red Cross in 1904. She was 82 years old. But Clara kept busy. She gave speeches. Clara fought for women's rights, too.

Clara Barton died on April 12, 1912. People have not forgotten her great achievements.

Americans have not forgotten humanitarian Clara Barton.

Today, more than one million Americans are Red Cross volunteers. They offer aid in many ways. The Red Cross trains people in health and safety. They collect blood for hospitals. Red Cross volunteers run homeless shelters and food pantries, too. Indeed, many people depend on the American Red Cross.

The American Red Cross has been around for more than 200 years.

Important Dates

December 25, 1821 Clara Barton is born.

1839 Clara begins teaching school.

1852 Clara opens a free public school in Bordentown, New Jersey.

1854 Clara moves to Washington, D.C. She works at the U.S. Patent Office.

1861 The Civil War begins. Clara starts gathering supplies for soldiers and nursing them.

August 1862 Clara brings supplies to hurt soldiers on the battlefield in Culpeper, Virginia.

March 1865 Clara begins searching for missing Civil War soldiers.

1870–1871 Clara joins the International Red Cross. She helps refugees during the Franco-Prussian War.

May 21, 1881 With Clara's help, the American Red Cross is formed. She is the president for 23 years.

April 12, 1912 Clara Barton dies at the age of 91.

Important Words

Civil War the United States war between the Northern and Southern states.

donate to give away something that helps others.

drought a long period of dry weather.

humanitarian someone who spends much of their life helping others.

refugee someone who leaves their home in search of a safe place.

volunteer someone who donates their time to help others.

Web Sites

To learn more about Clara Barton, visit ABDO Publishing Company on the World Wide Web at www.abdopub.com. Web sites about Clara Barton are featured on our Book Links page. These links are routinely monitored and updated to provide the most current information available.

Index